THE QUEENS

THE QUEENS

Normand Chaurette

Translated by Linda Gaboriau

Coach House Press   Toronto

Published with the assistance of the Canada Council, the Department of Communications, the Ontario Arts Council and the Ontario Ministry of Culture and Communications.

Editor for the Press: Robert Wallace
Cover Design: Orbit {Gary Stüber}
Cover Illustration: Janet Woolley
Printed in Canada

COACH HOUSE PRESS
401 (rear) Huron Street
Toronto, Canada
M5S 2G5

Canadian Cataloguing in Publication Data
Chaurette, Normand, 1954-
    [Reines. English]
    The queens
A play.
Translation of: Les Reines.
ISBN 0-88910-448-4
I. Title. II. Title: Reines. English.
PS855.H38R4513 1992   C842'.54   C92-095428-6
PQ3919.2.C48R4513 1992

to André Brassard

CONTENTS

FOREWORD

I love this play.

To write a foreword for the publication of *The Queens* is like re-vealing a love letter or describing to you lovely strangers an experience I can only have faith you will recognize when reading.

The Queens is a mystery; a mid-winter night's dream. Its brave vision and unique voice cut through the limited notions of history and finite reality and embrace the difficult terrain of poetry, ritual and the subconscious. This text is insistently poetic and strangely ambiguous, yet always alluring. These are words which dare you to speak them aloud. Images which never explain themselves, never illustrate, but express the mystery of living, dying and, perhaps, what lies beyond.

I love this play.

It is not a work of literature alone. Like all good mysteries, *The Queens* encourages us to draw upon other sources, people and experiences to derive its meaning, to solve the crime, to achieve enlightenment. Yet, as with mystery, so much of the reader's reward lies in the experience of discovery rather than in reaching its end. Normand understands implicitly that endings are but beginnings, and so the mystery continues and gathers power in its constant unfolding.

Poor shadows. Painted queens. A dream of what we were. A breath. A bubble.

I love this play.

The tower in *The Queens*, like the Tower of the Tarot, is a place of ambition built on false premises. It is built with the stones of tradition and the wrongful use of personal will. On the Tower card lightning bolts crash down from the heavens; the crown of materialistic thought falls. The lightning also represents the Divine destroying evil while purifying and refining what is good. A man and a woman fall from their tower of security after a blinding glimpse of truth. In the iconography of the Tarot the Tower signifies the Cosmic consciousness struggling to break through material ambitions, to bring them down in order to build again: *change, conflict, catastrophe, overthrow of existing ways of life, old notions upset, disruption will bring enlightenment.*

Sorrow admits society.

The Queens is much more than a re-examination of Shakespeare's *Richard III*, or a backstage pastiche on the goings-on in 1483. It's a re-vision of history: Shakespeare's queens in a dream of themselves, an imagining of our world through the glass of time. It captures those brilliant flashes of truth just as everything falls. Like dreams the text plays with our mythology and assumptions and gives substantial credence to the imagination in the face of injustice. Are the babes alive or dead? Is Anne Dexter real? How did she lose her hands? Why is George sequestered in the storage cellars? All these questions which are unanswerable, yet full of many possibilities—all are part of the mystery.

This is a play for actresses. It is a gift. And each actress that encounters it takes on its challenges in the personal and professional realms. It inspires creativity in its playing. We have found in rehearsal that the mystery is most profoundly expressed in the simple connections and in the most immediate. A daughter who confronts her mother's lack of recognition. A French queen who constantly leaves the English only to return. Women who struggle against a dying patriarchy and who will be changed forever by its collapse. The dream of reigning in the crowning glory of life for ten seconds just before death. Losing one's children. A sense of past lives before the World. All resonances personal, political, psychological and cultural swirl in the babble of the snowstorm that begins the play.

In all this mystery avoid the temptation to work at its meaning. Let the play work on you, lovely stranger; its rewards are life-changing.

Thank you Normand and Linda.

I love this play.

Peter Hinton, Toronto, October 1992

THE QUEENS

Les Reines was first produced by Théâtre d'aujourd'hui and premiered in Montreal on January 18, 1991 with the following cast:

ANNE DEXTER, Pol Pelletier
ANNE WARWICK, Linda Sorgini
ISABEL WARWICK, Élise Guilbault
QUEEN MARGARET, Michelle Rossignol
QUEEN ELIZABETH, Marthe Turgeon
DUCHESS OF YORK, Andrée Lachapelle

Director: André Brassard
Set and Costume Designer: Mérédith Caron
Lighting Designer: Manon Choinière
Assistant Director: Claude Lemelin
Assistant Set and Costume Designer: Jacqueline Rousseau
Stage Manager: Ann-Marie Corbeil

The Queens was first produced by Canadian Stage Company and received its English-language premiere in Toronto on November 6, 1992 with the following cast:

ANNE DEXTER, Denise Clarke
ANNE WARWICK, Jennifer Morehouse
ISABEL WARWICK, Siobhan McCormick
QUEEN MARGARET, Tanja Jacobs
QUEEN ELIZABETH, Margot Dionne
DUCHESS OF YORK, Marion Gilsenan

Director: Peter Hinton
Set and Costume Designer: John Ferguson
Music and Original Score: Marsha Coffey
Lighting Designer: Oliver Merk
Choreography: Denise Clarke
Assistant Director: Hans Engel
Stage Manager: Maria Popoff
Apprentice Stage Manager: Anne Marie McConney

The English translation was first workshopped at the Banff Playwrights' Colony in May 1991 under the direction of Kim McCaw.

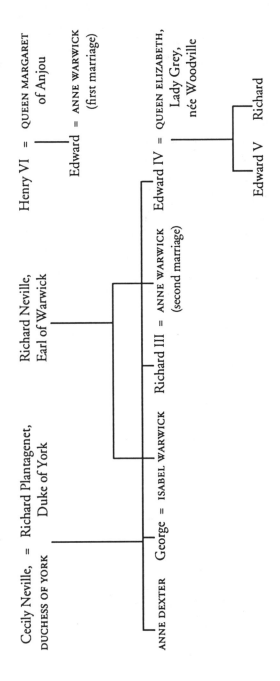

House of York

House of Lancaster

Cecily Neville, = Richard Plantagenet,
DUCHESS OF YORK   Duke of York

Richard Neville,
Earl of Warwick

Henry VI = QUEEN MARGARET
of Anjou

Edward = ANNE WARWICK
(first marriage)

Edward IV = QUEEN ELIZABETH,
Lady Grey,
née Woodville

Edward V   Richard

ANNE DEXTER   George = ISABEL WARWICK   Richard III = ANNE WARWICK
(second marriage)

Dramatis Personae

[in order of appearance]

ANNE DEXTER, sister of Edward, George and Richard
ANNE WARWICK, future Queen of England
ISABEL WARWICK, her sister, George's wife
QUEEN MARGARET, former Queen of England
QUEEN ELIZABETH, Queen of England, Edward's wife
DUCHESS OF YORK, mother of ANNE DEXTER, Edward, George
    and Richard

The action takes place in London in 1483.

BABBLE OF THE QUEENS

— Were you going out?
— I was on my way down.
— He came in downstairs.
— I've been upstairs.
— I'm leaving, farewell.
— You too?
— Where are you going?
— Shall we go up.
— Elevate myself above the world.
— Farewell.
— Where are you going down there?
— Do stay.
— I'm taking everything I need.
— Farewell.
— Farewell.
— Take care.
— London is disappearing before our very eyes.
— Ignore me.
— The most astonishing thing now ...
— Majesty!
— Silence.
— She defends who she is.
— Farewell.
— No, who she was!
— She gives with one hand.
— She exclaims:

— You were saying?

— With the other, she denies it.

— 'O deare sweet England!'

— She throws herself upon you.

— Dear children, I adore you!

— What? George?

— Edward.

— Not far from London

— Ailing flocks

— Plague the merchants

— Who negotiate

— Edward …

— Year after year

— The wind carries bad seed

— Which has lowered

— George …

— The price of stable animals

— Believe me …

— Our herds graze on it …

— … Anne Dexter

— … and develop malformations

— Seventy lambs …

— Stags and does …

— … are said to have contaminated the Thames

— … were found dead

— Everything lies fallow

— The ewes cannot be fattened

— This storm …

— The hounds who used to play

— Cower

— … is the worst

— And even the most gluttonous

— Refuse all nourishment.

— Believe me, Anne Dexter.
— George?
— I want to be damned.
— If peace.
— Reigns one day.
— Over our island.

[*The queens wander by;* ANNE WARWICK *stops* ANNE DEXTER]

ANNE AND ISABEL, SISTERS OF THE HOUSE OF WARWICK

ANNE WARWICK Believe me, Anne Dexter
  This storm is the worst
  We have known
  For years on end
  Have you walked north
  Facing the wind?
  I'd have bet two pennies
  That Queen Elizabeth
  Would be blown away
  Like a snowflake in the gale
  The wind always harasses her Majesty
  It resents her as vehemently as a sworn enemy
  Do you remember
  When we last went hawking
  I was certain she'd start
  Spinning like our waterfowl
  Over the marshes
  And how high
  your brother's falcons were gliding!
  And how vigilantly
  Richard observes his birds
  As if searching himself
  To capture their mechanism
  So he might rise flesh and blood
  Towards the heavens
  He who has such trouble
  Walking two steps without limping!
  No, Anne Dexter
  'Tis not his lameness
  Which makes me laugh

When Richard accosts me
In front of everyone
Those are infernal moments
When I force myself to laugh
I don't want to vex him
More than nature already has
Even though what he says
Is as lame as his person.
For this reason
I always wait till he has taken a step
Eastward
Before turning on my heels
And heading
Westward.
How tiny
The globe seems to me
So often do we meet
Face to face
Oh it isn't really
Richard who taunts me
As much as their majesties
Scarcely impressed by my efforts
To ward off his ill intentions
And they wag their tongues
Against my reputation—
They go so far as to unite
In a vast opinion
Claiming that my acts
Do naught but approve him.
You alone Anne Dexter
Never speak a defamatory
Word against me
When I mention to the queens

Your neutral approbation
They reply that your thoughts are unhealthy
Then they divide into pairs
Attacking one another
Though always in agreement
On the wherefore of their attacks.
You and I are united
In the anarchy of umbrage
You for the bad feelings
You inspire in this household
And I for my moods
All too prompt or so they claim meanly
To encourage Richard
They are convinced
That he covets the throne
And that once his wife
I shall be Queen of England.
I assure myself: King Edward is alive
Though he entered again this morning
Another phase of his agony
And as for George
The other brother you'd have to lose
Before I might reign
George too
Is still alive
But consider where their deaths
Might lead me:
Edward and George once gone
I become queen in no time.
This reign frightens me if only you knew
More than the idea of marrying Richard
Who's not as brutal as he is crippled
And less crippled at that

Than your family would have us believe.
Who amongst us really saw
Those famous teeth appear in his jaw
Barely two hours after birth
There are those who say
That he came into this world
With the sole goal of biting us.
Be frank
Has Richard ever bitten you?
He bites into beef
What could be more natural
When one considers, just think
How certain kings endowed with stomachs
More fragile than his
In order to appease God knows what appetite
Devoured their spouses?
No Anne Dexter
The idea of reigning o'er this island
Is unbearable
Terrifies me
'Tis a bad dream.
Queen Elizabeth has given birth
To two children who should inherit the crown
These births would relieve me
If the climate prevailing in this palace
Did not resemble
The atmosphere which assails London
Never have their majesties
Known such agitation
I need only meet them
At the foot of a staircase
To sense that I am as undesirable
As your brother Richard in person

If I close my eyes
I can see their lips speaking
Reproaches which reach me
Like the rumble of the surf
At night when I try to forget the day
And I can see them climb
From throne to throne
In the midst of cries and whispers ...
'Beware Anne Warwick
He is capable of anything
To conquer you:
Walks in the woods
Racing on horseback
After the horses will come the lakes
And the Thames
Then he'll offer you ships
Enormous vessels
He'll tell you that trade and commerce
Are yours for the asking
He'll offer you Ireland
The metals of the earth
The peaks of the icebergs
The course of the stars
Whether they shine in the East
The West or the North
And the South?
What South?
The South established on the globe
There is no South
England is in the North
Oh the northern vegetation!
The white climate of the Empire!
Anne Warwick

How often must I tell you
Not to walk like that
Your mouth wide open?'

[ISABEL WARWICK *enters, carrying* QUEEN ELIZABETH *'s babies*]

ISABEL WARWICK Stand up Sister of Warwick
Raise your brow
Frail but glorious
Undauntable
And take a deep breath
The queens are calling you
Can't you hear them?
Perhaps, but you believed
It was the wind.
Have you seen the weather unleashed on London?
The confusion of noises
Makes me fear so
I am seeking a refuge
A resting place for these babes.
ANNE WARWICK Leave them in my care
I shall be kind and loving.
ISABEL WARWICK [*turning away*] If you intend to give them to Richard ...
ANNE WARWICK [*indicating* ANNE DEXTER] I heard her
She can talk, Sister of Warwick.
ISABEL WARWICK Anne Dexter?
She found her tongue?
To better despise us out loud
Treating us like intruders?
So she can insist upon humiliating you
Through defamation
So many attempts to make us forget
That every member of her family
Is maimed, mute or limbless.

ANNE WARWICK Nonetheless Sister of Warwick
She spoke the other day
And I saw the look of horror
Come over the Duchess of York.
I am sure it is she, her mother,
Who has forbidden her to speak.
I shouldn't be at all surprised
If George your husband
Were to succeed himself one day ...

ISABEL WARWICK George ... Ha! He too might speak!
After all the years we've dreamed of it!
The future King of England would say:
'How ambitious you are Isabel
You had a hankering for monarchy
And you married me in silence
Knowing full well our hounds
Were more brilliant than I
And thanks to me you are rising
Isabel you are rising
To the equal of the queens.'

[*Beat*]

No, Sister of Warwick
George and Anne Dexter
When they were no older than you
Travelled down the Thames
To the estuary
God knows what there did happen
That upon their return
To all the questions put to them
Never another word, another sound
Came out of their mouths.
They were hungry that day

On the shore at low tide
And they devoured silence.

ANNE WARWICK Is the mouth of the Thames
So far from London
That one can encounter silence
And take it into oneself forever?

ISABEL WARWICK 'Tis a full day's journey to there
The queens go every Friday
I've made the trip three times
We leave early in the morning
Quietly, without alerting the kings
Dressed in old cloaks
Hiding our faces behind veils
There the sky and the horizon
Become one
We hide behind the rocks and jetties
And we can observe them
From nigh as close as I to you
The pilgrims who come ashore
And collapse
Their garments soaked
They emerge from the fog
And fall to the ground midst the seaweed
Poverty reaches us from the end of the world
The Spaniards, they are the ones
Who bring misery to our shores
And who kneel to kiss the sand
And roll towards the rocks
Right there
Almost at our feet.

ANNE WARWICK That fateful day when George and Anne Dexter
Travelled to the shore
Was it such pilgrims

Who spied them
And reported
What they saw?
Why have they sequestered George
Down in the storage cellars?
Why have they punished his sister?
She must have had lovely hands.

ISABEL WARWICK Yes—they ought to buy some for her.
Edward is on his deathbed, George will reign
And once queen
I shall introduce steel
To save bronze;
I shall give her hands of steel.

ANNE WARWICK Provided George
Rises to the throne.
But should he die, Sister of Warwick?
When I enter Edward's chamber
I see them all gathered
The archbishops, the pages
And I hear them
They speak only words of praise
And approbation for Richard's resolution
Seeking to eliminate George.

ISABEL WARWICK But if George were already dead ...

ANNE WARWICK George? And who would have already killed him?

ISABEL WARWICK It would suffice to spread the news
And the assassins will abandon their plans.

ANNE WARWICK Richard gave the assassins their orders
For the middle of this night.

ISABEL WARWICK Ah—for the middle of the night ...

[ISABEL WARWICK *goes to leave with the children*]

ANNE WARWICK Where are you going?

ISABEL WARWICK Downstairs, to the cellars—
They will be safer there than here
In this hall where the walls
Have eyes to watch us
And ears to listen
And if I am to believe you Sister of Warwick
They well might decide to speak.

[*She exits*]

VOICE OF QUEEN ELIZABETH Farewell my king
My dragon of hope
Farewell my sole echelon
You return to the earth
Along the road of your life reversed
Meeting no more pitfalls
Than you encountered hitherto
Let me point the way to slumber
Anchored beyond the horizon
Open your eyes that they may drink in
Enough light for kingdom come
Descend to the wellsprings
Let your memory be the navigator
Sink your soul in the reflection
Of those waters which quench thirst
Our life was but a shadow
Cast upon the dunes
Our dreams have fled far from us
To the depths of the springs.
Anne Warwick
What was that commotion in the stairway?

EFFIGY OF EDWARD

The bells strike noon. QUEEN MARGARET *enters*

QUEEN MARGARET Edward in supremacy
  Rent by the wheel of his pain
  Edward our sovereign
  Our lord our everything
  Our King Edward is dead
  His death was as long
  As his reign was brief
  The day had barely risen
  First his feet were overcome
  While in the centre of his chest
  His heart was prey to invisible animals
  Seeking to feed off blood
  Just before the stroke of seven
  The king lost one of his hands
  Which fell from the weaker
  Of his arms
  And rolled to the foot of his bed
  Some fifteen twenty minutes later
  His left eye splattered
  In icy trickles
  Down his ashen cheek
  Hurrying towards an end
  Still uncertain for the queen
  To whom the dying man's
  Cracked lips mouthed:
  'Why leave time
  Why leave time?'
  Upon these words His Majesty's
  Mouth died

Sealing his lips forever.
Yet they open again
As the tower strikes eight
And behold the foam
Of potions now rejected
By the esophagus and stomach
Which continue to survive
The poisonous blood
All the veins and vessels
expire one by one
And close to the hour of nine
They become so many dams
Rerouting the humours
Which in their fight for life
Take refuge in the forehead
A forehead already blackened
By the design of hope
Where the wish for an impossible
Cure tries to assert itself.
Ten o'clock, he is suffering.
Eleven o'clock, he is suffering.
'O king,' murmurs the queen,
'You only appear to be dying.'
But Elizabeth's lies
Are insufficient cure:
Rather than lessening the pain
Suffered by the dead man
The queen's tears
Aggravate the infection
And prolong
Till half eleven
The leftovers
Of a life

Torn asunder
While the king moans that
The unknown terrifies him.
Five to noon:
'You are afraid of the unknown,'
Replies the queen crying
'But what shall you do in the beyond?'
Four minutes pass
And at the stroke of noon
His hair falls from his head
''Tis noon, Your Majesty'
'King's orders—flee oblivion at all costs'
And it is apparent that the body
Is indeed a vast universe
While the moon
Draws the soul into her rays
And while the archbishops
And the pages murmur:
'May God bless this soul
And preserve ours
From the Hell that Queen Elizabeth
Will impose upon us shortly.'

THE MOON — LA LUNE

QUEEN ELIZABETH *enters, dishevelled*

QUEEN ELIZABETH He's alive! Edward is alive!

[She falls]

Our chambers have become
A veritable marketplace
There are attendants
And people I have never seen
Noisy and disorderly
Perhaps I am in their eyes
Merely a merchant's wife
Like these scroungers
So satisfied with their status
Who dare utter in my chambers
Their unsolicited opinions
But if the king regains his health
Tomorrow they shall know who I am
And they will bow and scrape
Before the strength, the assurance
And the simplicity of my courage.
'Tis true that in the meanwhile
Nary a soul seems aware
Of the unnatural state
Into which I've been plunged
I had to shout to stop their chatter
They all stared at me aghast
And in that silence—surprise—
The inert mass
Stretched out beneath our gaze
Comes to life with a start

And demands that his testament be reopened.
I like many others believed
That he was indeed dead
Having succeeded in convincing him
That it was I who was departing
For a life beyond this world
Forever
I rather than he
And I had already bid
An infinite number of farewells
To everything I was prepared to lose
My ornaments both plain and regal
My hounds who quiver at the forest's edge
All the customary leavetaking
A majestic farewell
To all that I preferred
From the humble to the grand
Springs, birds, earth, moon
And pearls of the deep sea.

[*She stands again*]

Anne Warwick
What was that commotion in the stairway?
ANNE WARWICK Pages have arrived
   Delivering a shipment of malmsey.
QUEEN ELIZABETH But today isn't Wednesday.
   What day is today?
ANNE WARWICK Thursday, Elevation Day.
QUEEN ELIZABETH Margaret, what day is today?
QUEEN MARGARET Elevation Day.
QUEEN ELIZABETH Then why this commerce?
ANNE WARWICK They could not come before this morning.
   Everything is arriving late

Due to the weather.

QUEEN ELIZABETH Is it really snowing, or was I dreaming?

ANNE WARWICK It is snowing Majesty
You remarked on it yourself
As you left the Abbey.

QUEEN ELIZABETH London was buried 'tis true
And I mentioned it to you
Yes it is snowing
That is why I remain stable
Upright I maintain my balance
In the air stripped of sentiment
Everything dwindles
Yet I feel no dizziness
You are there
As if you were about to dissolve before my eyes
And of you Margaret
I can only see a poor painted queen.

QUEEN MARGARET A fine glimpse of yourself
You are beginning to leave the throne.

QUEEN ELIZABETH Poor Margaret!
My throne is not yet vacant
For if it were you would already be ensconced.

QUEEN MARGARET Poor Elizabeth!
From this day on sorrow will assail you
And lie with you in your bed.

QUEEN ELIZABETH Poor Margaret!
Your sorrow scorches your eyes
When you contemplate yourself every morning in your mirror.

QUEEN MARGARET And whom do I see?
My reflection weeps when looking at me
For it knows, true as it is
That I am not false.

QUEEN ELIZABETH You have always despised

Our despair and our sorrow.

QUEEN MARGARET The sorrows of the world weigh little
　　Compared to mine
　　Famines and blights
　　The networks of the plague
　　These are sorrows visible
　　To all peoples
　　My personal sorrow is boredom.

QUEEN ELIZABETH [*dumbstruck*] But are you not in London?

QUEEN MARGARET Poor Elizabeth!
　　Where else might I be?

QUEEN ELIZABETH How should I know? Anjou, Scotland
　　Or the Asia of your plans
　　For which you bade us
　　Farewell yesterday eve
　　Long farewell greetings which we listened to standing
　　Patiently
　　How we suffered
　　Till we finally bade you to tie the knot
　　But rather than conclude
　　You began anew from the beginning.
　　Anne Warwick, surely I did not dream that?

QUEEN MARGARET Poor Elizabeth!
　　The winds had already begun
　　To howl over London
　　And you yourself said
　　That it was wiser to remain than to depart.

QUEEN ELIZABETH I said that?

QUEEN MARGARET Mocking me, yes, you said that.
　　And you called me a cockatrice, a clovenhoof—

QUEEN ELIZABETH [*remembering*] Clovenhoof!

QUEEN MARGARET Clovenhoof, foreign queen
　　Hydromedusa—and wet hen.

QUEEN ELIZABETH Anne Warwick
  Are you the one to whom I entrusted my children?
ANNE WARWICK No Majesty
  They were in my sister's arms.
QUEEN ELIZABETH Where is she?
  If Richard is to take them
  He will have to tear them away from me.
ANNE WARWICK She went downstairs
  At the very moment I learned
  That the king was dead.
QUEEN ELIZABETH Who said that ...
QUEEN MARGARET I thought he was dead.
QUEEN ELIZABETH But he is alive—Edward is alive
  And has consented to the distribution of benefits
  The Woodvilles, I first amongst them
  Are in the process of inheriting.
  The treasure of England
  Rightfully belongs to England.
QUEEN MARGARET England land of meadows
  For you were born in the meadows
  And you come from the stables.
QUEEN ELIZABETH Shepherdess, humble, simpleminded
  But native to our isle
  Where the goats are English
  Where the lambs are English
  Where the weavers are English
  Where the pastures are English
  Where the streets are English
  Where the days are English
  Where the counties are English
  Where the sky, the birds, the snow
  The tools, the coins ...
  Anne Warwick

Go see to settling the deliveries.

ANNE WARWICK Yes Majesty.

QUEEN ELIZABETH I

I came looking for something.

ANNE WARWICK Your children Majesty.

QUEEN ELIZABETH My children!

Stand guard at the doors.

And let me know

Any news from the king's quarters.

[*She exits in the direction of the storage cellars*]

THE FURNACE

QUEEN MARGARET [*to* QUEEN ELIZABETH] Hurry
  Richard is probably preparing to eat them.
ANNE WARWICK Eat them?
  I don't think he wants to eat them.
  Should he, he'd better not count on me
  To surrender them.
QUEEN MARGARET So Richard did ask you for them?
ANNE WARWICK But not to roast them.
QUEEN MARGARET Richard has jurisdiction
  Over the furnace in the cellars
  In less than one hour
  He can stoke a fire
  Hot enough to roast the Earth.
ANNE WARWICK Is this furnace so enormous?
QUEEN MARGARET So huge you can take a stroll in it.
ANNE WARWICK You have seen it yourself?
  Do you go there sometimes?
QUEEN MARGARET More often than one thinks
  To escape from all of you.
  I so detest my fate
  A furnace seems refreshing.
ANNE WARWICK And now where are you going?
QUEEN MARGARET I have resolved to leave London
  I am leaving today.
ANNE WARWICK You're leaving London forever?
  What? In this freezing cold?
QUEEN MARGARET Consider me long gone
  Here life is not worth living.
ANNE WARWICK But so many times
  You have told us you were leaving.
QUEEN MARGARET My farewell greetings

39

Have never been more sincere.

ANNE WARWICK Farewell then
  Even if you stay.

QUEEN MARGARET [*impassive*] Alas no, I am leaving
  I have suffered too long
  I shall seek exile in France
  In the fair county of Anjou
  Where I was queen in the monarchy.

  [*She embraces* ANNE WARWICK]

ANNE WARWICK Don't forget to go downstairs
  And embrace my sister.

QUEEN MARGARET She is not the best
  Of my memories of this isle.

ANNE WARWICK Did she wrong you in some way?

QUEEN MARGARET Never mind—what's the sense?

ANNE WARWICK She spoke of you to me
  Just yesterday, with kindness.

QUEEN MARGARET Can she be kind on occasion?
  What does this word mean?

ANNE WARWICK She doesn't waste her time
  Spreading idle defamation.

QUEEN MARGARET Just what does she spread then?
  Sarcasm?
  And at whose expense!

ANNE WARWICK She simply said
  You were not very happy.

QUEEN MARGARET Indeed a fine example
  To illustrate the reversal of fate
  And who reaps happiness
  By quoting another woman's despair?

ANNE WARWICK If you only knew ...

QUEEN MARGARET Be still: I know everything.

ANNE WARWICK ... How my sister is to be reckoned with
    In the royal hierarchy.
QUEEN MARGARET Hardly surprising since this domain
    Now belongs to the two of you!
ANNE WARWICK It remains open to you.
QUEEN MARGARET So that I might leave!
    Goodness you speak
    As if you were offering me alms
    And I need only
    Thank you
    For feeling totally humiliated
    I who was pride incarnate
    When England and Scotland
    Knelt at my feet.
    Farewell, this memory
    Which returns abruptly
    Makes me wish
    I had never laid eyes on England.
ANNE WARWICK You mustn't take it with you.
QUEEN MARGARET If forgetting were so simple
    'Tis your entire island
    That I'd erase from my brow.
ANNE WARWICK Would you go so far as to forget
    The joy of having been queen?
QUEEN MARGARET Yes dear Lord
    If forgetting could relieve the pain
    of seeing another
    Enjoy her reign in my stead.
ANNE WARWICK Another whose turn has come
    To lose all.
QUEEN MARGARET Once she has lost all
    Everything, including her children
    I want her to regain everything

So she might lose it all again.

ANNE WARWICK Such cruelty.

QUEEN MARGARET Cruelty? And what did the Warwicks do to me?

ANNE WARWICK Yet it is the Yorkists
Who sentenced you to the stake.

QUEEN MARGARET Ah the stake!
I had never been
So politically content
Yes there I was the supplicant
My arms outstretched, begging them
To put the torches to my skin
Dashed hopes
I sought it with too much passion
And you even considered
Denying me access to the furnace
For fear that lawfully
I would tend to my own burning.

ANNE WARWICK Leave, 'tis best.

QUEEN MARGARET You preferred to disobey your own laws.

ANNE WARWICK I was only twelve years old ...

QUEEN MARGARET ... Yet you signed
In an ink
Which spattered the other signatures.
I can still see your incredible *W*'s
On my death warrant
As if the name Warwick contained at least a thousand.

ANNE WARWICK [*offended*] There were only two.

QUEEN MARGARET Along with your sister's
That made all too many
Oh yes Anne and Isabel
Sisters of the House of Warwick
You signed a procuration
Which made your hatred of me lawful

And when that fateful morning
You saw me return from the Abbey
You fell to the ground
In the palace entrance
On bended knee
You bade me good day
Though your fingers
Were still stained with ink.

ANNE WARWICK They had forced me
I wasn't very old and ...

QUEEN MARGARET ... And you were already
The most corrupt of them all.

ANNE WARWICK Worse corruptions are yet to come.

QUEEN MARGARET Name them.

ANNE WARWICK I can't name them all.

QUEEN MARGARET Those that you know.

ANNE WARWICK Richard.

QUEEN MARGARET Richard!

ANNE WARWICK He asked me ...

QUEEN MARGARET Asked you what?

ANNE WARWICK To marry him—
And I said yes.

QUEEN MARGARET You said yes!
Like your sister!
One marries an ass
The other a toad
The perfect government!
At least the subjects will laugh—
Heavens you want me to stay!
And how can one give credence
To all your lies?
Anne Warwick!
You even lie to us about your age!

ANNE WARWICK [*tense*] I am twelve years old!
QUEEN MARGARET You were already twelve
  When I was elevated to the throne!
ANNE WARWICK I am twelve years old.
  Twelve, the number twelve.
QUEEN MARGARET Aaaah! Enough!
  Twelve years old
  My Lord I believe you but nonetheless:
  You couldn't possibly
  Wreak so much havoc
  In so few years.
ANNE WARWICK Where are you going?
QUEEN MARGARET Downstairs.
ANNE WARWICK But aren't you leaving?
QUEEN MARGARET I'm going to fetch my things—half of everything
  To be found in the cellars belongs to me.

  [*She exits*]

ANNE WARWICK Wait, I said yes
  But that was in my dreams
  I couldn't see the end of the nights
  His eternal request
  Eastward—westward
  Wherever I went he'd arrive head on
  When I needed only
  To consent to Richard ...

  [ISABEL WARWICK *enters*]

  ... to release my soul from his nights
  Sister of Warwick!

One o'clock

ISABEL WARWICK George!
ANNE WARWICK George?
ISABEL WARWICK I saw him ...
    His blood ... his eyes ...
ANNE WARWICK What?
ISABEL WARWICK George, inanimate.
ANNE WARWICK An illusion.
ISABEL WARWICK I saw him!
ANNE WARWICK Be calm, he is alive.
ISABEL WARWICK Dead.
ANNE WARWICK No.
ISABEL WARWICK I assure you he is dead.
    Just go downstairs
    You'll see the bloodstains.
ANNE WARWICK Bloodstains?
    Then someone else killed him
    They were supposed to drown him
    In a cask of malmsey.
ISABEL WARWICK They bled him to death first
    Then brought him where they store the wine.
ANNE WARWICK What?
    That commotion in the stairway?
    It wasn't the pages?
ISABEL WARWICK Run and tell Richard
    That they've already killed George.

[ANNE WARWICK *exits in the direction of the castle*]

ISABEL WARWICK Queen, me.
    Queen at the centre

My subjects gathered round.

[QUEEN ELIZABETH *enters*]

QUEEN ELIZABETH [*to* ISABEL WARWICK] You had them just a while ago.
   Where are they? Who is looking after them?
ISABEL WARWICK [*evasively*] My sister Anne Warwick.
QUEEN ELIZABETH Anne Warwick ...
   Ahhh! Not your sister?
   Oh no not her!
   We must catch up with her
   She's capable of delivering them
   Into the arms of Richard
   I know he asked for them
   I know he wants to kill them.
ISABEL WARWICK Tolerance Majesty.
QUEEN ELIZABETH Rumours abound
   They're after your husband
   They're after my children.
   Born barely a day ago
   And we've already lost them
   At least twenty times!

[ANNE WARWICK *enters*]

ANNE WARWICK [*under her breath*] Calamity Majesty.
QUEEN ELIZABETH [*she braces herself*] Ah!
ANNE WARWICK I saw her just ahead of me
   Like a ghost who takes an hour
   For every step taken.
   Here she comes, shortly.
QUEEN ELIZABETH Oh, mercy, not again!

[*The* DUCHESS OF YORK *enters*]

DUCHESS OF YORK I took my leave of Edward

To come to bid you all a noble
Sincere and sovereign good day
May God be with you
And bless the sky
In the throes of snow
And wind which assail us.
My dear daughters-in-law
From the Houses of Warwick and Woodville ...
[*turning to* ANNE DEXTER] ... And you
Lovely stranger sojourning in the city of London
[*at large*] Hail to my faithful companions
With indulgent ears
Without whom I'd be left alone
To listen to myself moan.
Entire cities have been known
To disappear from the globe
We heard voices predicting it.

ISABEL WARWICK Predicting what?

DUCHESS OF YORK The return.

ISABEL WARWICK What return?

DUCHESS OF YORK The return of the Deluge.

ISABEL WARWICK It isn't raining, it's snowing.

DUCHESS OF YORK And blowing.

QUEEN ELIZABETH Yes London is in the process of disappearing.

DUCHESS OF YORK London has disappeared.

QUEEN ELIZABETH Yet we are visible?

DUCHESS OF YORK For we are too warm alas
    The snow cannot last on us
    Who remain here intact
    While our isle has become no more
    Than a great deserted veil.

ISABEL WARWICK How is his Grace?

DUCHESS OF YORK Poorly—

Nothing lends itself to anything now
Our heads are mere whirlwinds
Of useless crystals
Which try to escape us
Like sharp shafts of light.
[*her eyes closed*] I am ninety-nine years old
And my skin is green
I came
Almost a century ago
To England
With, as my sole claim to glory,
A glistening pearl
In the palm of my hand.
On the arm of this Empire's
Lord Protector.
I dominated the Court
Lost in his grandeur
Being at once himself
His mistress and his shadow.
I defied Christianity
In order to be his companion
And I gave birth to Richard
Among my sons
Whose most merciless crime
Is to have never murdered my illusions.
And as for Edward, on his eternal deathbed ...
QUEEN ELIZABETH ... He awaits me at his bedside
Sovereign Duchess—farewell.
DUCHESS OF YORK Yes Edward enjoys the privilege of dying
For him, nothing can wait—
Farewell then.

[QUEEN ELIZABETH *exits in the direction of the castle*]

DUCHESS OF YORK Anne Warwick!
  A child I cradled in my arms just yesterday!
  How time does dissipate us!
  Where are your beautiful clear eyes?
  Come here and tell me how
  You suffer at the hands of the queens—
  They slander, they are unkind.
ANNE WARWICK Prodigious Duchess
  Was George downstairs this morning?
DUCHESS OF YORK Yes he was
  Victorious in battle
  His eyes almost closed staring
  At unending rivers.
ANNE WARWICK Then he was alive?
DUCHESS OF YORK As alive as a star in the heavens.
ANNE WARWICK What time was it?
ISABEL WARWICK [*pulling* ANNE *away*] Why all these questions?
  She's delirious and you listen to her!
  Be off
  Be off to see Richard.

[ANNE WARWICK *and* ISABEL WARWICK *exit in the direction of the castle*]

DUCHESS OF YORK Anne, are you leaving?
  No, wait—do take me with you …

CHINA

QUEEN MARGARET *enters with her baggage and the children*

QUEEN MARGARET I am leaving for China
For the peaks of fabulous Asia
These children will see the other side of the world
Where the sun shines bright.
DUCHESS OF YORK Let me see
A few wrinkles, here and there
Make it hard to remember that you were
Scarcely more than a few days ago
Or so it seems—queen.
QUEEN MARGARET I know by heart
How many teeth you have left
And your hair—
Wait let me count them
Try as I might
I cannot see more than eight
Provided one splits
Each hair into four
As for your wrinkles
They've frightened away our songbirds
And if I had only half
So many on my face
I would have fled ages ago
To some place on this earth
Where I could live
Far from the light of day.
DUCHESS OF YORK If I hadn't always
Frightened away the birds of prey
They would never cease to circle
Round your putrid lives!

QUEEN MARGARET Putrid am I?

   Today perhaps ...

DUCHESS OF YORK In those days as well.

QUEEN MARGARET In those days in the county of Anjou

   I was hale and hardy

   A shameless beauty

   Of boundless charm.

DUCHESS OF YORK You should have stayed in France

   Queen of the county monarchy.

   Give me those children.

QUEEN MARGARET They have no mother

   I'm taking them with me.

   [*spreading out her baggage*] I'm also taking my slippers

   My boots and my kettles

   You have two or three bonnets

   Which belong to me—keep them

   I have however taken

   My sheepskin stoles from your hutch.

   There are advantages to my departure

   Tucked among the ivory corsets

   I found a chamois glove

   Worn by Queen Eleanor

   Who lived to be eighty-two

   I do wish I could find the other

   In France people would pay a fortune for the pair.

   By the way, did you know that I was an archduchess?

   I was unaware myself

   On my warrant of accession to the throne

   It's written black on white: archduchess.

   You'll notice in my chest

   I've left some jewels

   I'm taking only these

   I've taken this vase

This lovely fabric
These fine metals
Pure bronze
Look at this aspergill
From my own christening
The Great Book of Wonders
And the *mappa mundi* of Syracuse
Which good King René
Received from Charles I of Anjou
Who received it from Pope Boniface
Who had received it in turn
From Marco Polo's mistress;
The proclamation of pardon
And the agenda of successions
I have a right to the papers of the monarchy
I am taking them with me
My powders and essences
My rags and my linens
So I can sleep on my journey
I shall abandon the rest here—
My illusions, my torments
And my sleepless nights
If I could leave my heartaches
I'd make you a present of them all.
Here, take my key
To remind you of the days
When you plotted against me.
You need only open my door
Throw back the carpet
And look carefully beneath the dust—
Just blow and see:
I have left my soul behind.

DUCHESS OF YORK What do you expect the future queens

To do with your soul?
Erected on tombs
This house is filled to the rafters
With forgotten souls.

[ISABEL WARWICK *enters*]

ISABEL WARWICK Why Madame d'Anjou!
Does all this belong to you?
For years now I've wondered
Who collects these old stockings
These old bits and pieces, all this clutter.
QUEEN MARGARET Clutter!
ISABEL WARWICK Must I conclude
Oblivious to the gusts and gales
You are preparing
Your impetuous departure for France?
QUEEN MARGARET Your countenance belies
How my departure taints your happiness.
ISABEL WARWICK My heart is broken
To see that you are leaving.
QUEEN MARGARET Certainly in my clutter I can find
Something to glue it together.
ISABEL WARWICK You'd do better to clear the floor
Today is Thursday.
I wish I could avoid it
But Thursday the laws are strict:
Nothing must interfere with the Elevation of the Queens.
QUEEN MARGARET [*devastated*] Rest assured
You won't have to elevate yourself midst my clutter.

[*She gathers up her clutter*]

ISABEL WARWICK I do envy your fortune.
QUEEN MARGARET My fortune, these old stockings?

ISABEL WARWICK With the ambiguity of the word fortune
    I am only referring
    To your strength and your admirable courage
    We all dream of leaving
    England is so dreary ...
    Thus in eight days time
    You'll have reconquered France?
QUEEN MARGARET China.
ISABEL WARWICK [*stoically*] China.
    And what will you do in China?
QUEEN MARGARET Continue to loathe the lot of you.
    I want to see how far one can take contempt
    However distant one might be.
ISABEL WARWICK And what about the throne?
    Mmmm ... hard to say.
QUEEN MARGARET The what? The throne?
    The throne! What throne?
ISABEL WARWICK The throne of the ... samurai why not!
    I assume he sits somewhere?
    There where you are going
    Isn't there always a throne to be usurped?
QUEEN MARGARET They have real families there ...
ISABEL WARWICK ... More vigilant than ours?
QUEEN MARGARET China is in safe hands.
ISABEL WARWICK And do the leisured queens
    The fallen empresses
    Have enough to eat among the mandarins?
QUEEN MARGARET As much as sisters
    Dissolute in their corruption.
ISABEL WARWICK As much as intruders!
    Farewell now, and forever
    Though dare I say 'forever'
    'Tis no way to measure time

We shall see by the length of your absence
How far the principle extends.

QUEEN MARGARET The principle cannot be extended
Whereas I shall go far.

ISABEL WARWICK Then once again I say farewell
And promise I shall think of you
If and when I find the respite
Midst the throes of the reign which awaits me.
Oh—it's almost two o'clock
I must run to dress
Give me back that chamois glove—
It belongs to me.

QUEEN MARGARET The glove of Queen Eleanor who lived to be eighty-two!

ISABEL WARWICK I've been searching for it for days now.
Come—give it back to me
It is part of the Warwick inheritance.

QUEEN MARGARET Do you have proof?

ISABEL WARWICK Isn't there a little *W*
Embroidered inside the cuff?
Wait ... here ... mmm ...

QUEEN MARGARET Only in France
Can you find these embroidered stitches.
It bears no resemblance
To your manufactured gloves.

ISABEL WARWICK That glove is mine.

QUEEN MARGARET Where is the *W?* Show it to me!

ISABEL WARWICK Mmmm ... there was one on the other glove
Wait, I'll run and fetch it.

[*She exits in the direction of the castle*]

QUEEN MARGARET And why not my corsets?
And my warrant of accession while you're at it!
And why not all my baggage?

You've taken everything else from me
My joys, my dignity
The lightheartedness of my youth
And now
You strip me of my memories ...
[*to the* DUCHESS OF YORK] Farewell forever.
I am leaving and I take with me more offences
Than any other woman here
Is capable of suffering.
DUCHESS OF YORK Leave the babes with me.
Think of Elizabeth's grief
The moment you set foot outside
They'll perish of the cold.
QUEEN MARGARET I shall be the wind who carries them away
Or I shall stay
So there—consider the exchange
The choice is yours
Either I depart with them
And promise never to return
Or I leave them with you
And linger here till your death.
DUCHESS OF YORK You commit yourself for little time
I would so like to see you
Far away from our isle
That if I didn't still have
A scrap of heart left in me
I would tell you to leave
With them forever.
QUEEN MARGARET Did you never love me then?
DUCHESS OF YORK Leave.
QUEEN MARGARET Tell me to stay
And I'll stay.
DUCHESS OF YORK This day has already begun

To see us disappear
London has buried itself
Our children are leaving for Asia
Edward is going to his grave
And the world is shrinking
Soon it shall be little more
Than a stitch of lace
Invisible in the infinite
Leave
Don't wait for me to die
Before you leave me.

QUEEN MARGARET Farewell then.

DUCHESS OF YORK Feed them with tender love, naught else.

QUEEN MARGARET Did you never love me, Cecily?

[*Silence*]

Farewell.

DUCHESS OF YORK Farewell.

[QUEEN MARGARET *exits with her baggage and the children*]

THE WORLD

Two o'clock

ANNE DEXTER Feed them
  With
  With
  Tender love
  Feed them
  With ... tender love!
  Yes
  Before everything comes toppling down
  In this single day
  We will have seen and heard
  Everything
  Our walls are crumbling
  Under the grip of frost
  We no longer know
  Whether it is day or night
  The king is collapsing
  And the universe along with him
  Our household is at the mercy
  Of the intruders from the House of Warwick
  And I hear my mother
  Utter the words 'tender love'
  Can I trust my ears?
  'Tender love'
  On my mother's lips!
  Look at me
  Look at me and say it again.
DUCHESS OF YORK I do not know you
  You have travelled round the world
  And since no one wanted you

You found refuge here in the city of London
Look where that has led us:
The city is disappearing from the globe.

ANNE DEXTER Yet you and I remain
Imperishable as we are
One hundred years, and you still insist upon living?
Spurred by bravery or fear?
And what if dead
You continue to hear us, George and me!

[ISABEL WARWICK *enters, a glove in her hand; surprised, she stands aside and listens*]

DUCHESS OF YORK You were born far from our dominion
And you cannot know who George is.
The most accomplished of my children
But stricken at the age of one
With a loss of judgement
Deprived forever of the power of speech.

ANNE DEXTER I have heard tell as well
Of a daughter among these brothers.
I often hear you reply
To those who inquire
The most extravagant stories—
It takes you hours
To explain that that girlchild
Was never born.

DUCHESS OF YORK I wanted to have her
But in the flesh she was never born.
This girl people speak of
Must be Anne Dexter—
But in fact she was a Spaniard
Who lied about her origins
Trying to pass for my daughter.

Did they tell you she is missing her hands?

ANNE DEXTER Yes

And that the extremities of her arms

Remained in your belly

You expedited into this world

An imperfect tool a breach of birth

And Anne wanders about lost forever

Like the memories in your soul.

DUCHESS OF YORK Search though I might

I cannot imagine who it is.

A boychild, I'd say Richard

But Anne?

Anne is the name of a child who doesn't exist.

ANNE DEXTER Then you must ask George

Quickly before he dies!

Though the sisters of Warwick

Speak as if he'd already been assassinated.

DUCHESS OF YORK He is alive.

ANNE DEXTER Then you must ask him who is Anne!

DUCHESS OF YORK What is the sense since he is mute?

ANNE DEXTER He need only hear me.

DUCHESS OF YORK Shut up.

He locked himself up in silence

And I alone could set him free.

ANNE DEXTER You alone?

DUCHESS OF YORK He would speak if I wished it.

ANNE DEXTER You?

DUCHESS OF YORK Yes I.

ANNE DEXTER Of course he has the thrust and the strength of a tree

And furthermore he would speak to you!

My mother gave birth to light

And she is hiding it—

The midnight sun blinded you

You preferred twilight
But even at nightfall
George continues to dazzle you
And you can no longer bear to see me soar.

DUCHESS OF YORK You cannot soar or dazzle
For you are not a star.

ANNE DEXTER But I have the brightness of a star
My head is bursting with a thousand stars
Dead many times but luminous
I intend now to drown you
In the torrents I've been holding back
Look at my mouth
You ordered me to silence
Look I am honest
Have you ever seen me
Address a single word to others?
But alone with you
I can speak.

DUCHESS OF YORK Be silent.

ANNE DEXTER How can you forbid me to speak?
Beware, beware the Duchess of York
What I am is full of words
Full of questions
Full of 'Tell me who is Anne?'
Full of 'Tell me who is George?'
And if they were to tell you he is dead?

DUCHESS OF YORK He is alive. He is alive.

ANNE DEXTER 'He is alive. He is alive.'
Of course, since he can speak.
He can speak if you so wish it!
And what does he say to you?
Gasps and groans
Sounds strung together

Words that cannot be found
In any lexicon.
DUCHESS OF YORK Many words he uses
Can be understood.
ANNE DEXTER Ha! An erudite man!
Why should I be astonished?
George was a sphere of love
But I reigned in his heart
Ah it must have been painful
To give way to his queen!
And you watched my hands
Trying to see, left or right
Which caressed most gently
George's sacred hair.
You felt that you recognized
Something you had never seen
And I know that many a time
You came to the estuary
Seeking a bit of lucidity
For your memory frayed
And tattered as the peninsulas.
You tried to discern in the dunes
The traces that the tides
Despite countless lunar cycles
Should never have erased.
How you searched
Signs became visible
They were ancient
You could see them all
Jean Sans Terre Jean Sans Chagrin
Jean Sans Herbage and Good King John
Their mistresses and their joys
Their momemts of oblivion

But not a trace of Anne nor George
It was too ancient
It was before time immemorial
You understood that we had been there first
And the world arrived afterwards
You were only our mother
But born after us—
Anne and George loved each other
Told each other all their longings
Openly before you
Before the Thames before the world.
Yes we loved each other
In the beginning you watched us
You saw us at the table
We were side by side
You watched us without understanding
But with a peaceful eye
Almost benevolent
You were moved to see us happy
Remember early on
You brought up Richard
To follow our example, George and me:
Who could better illustrate
The peace in our household?
Yet only months later
This peace had lasted too long
In your mind full of suspicion
You had to understand
And decipher something unknown
Which bore more and more
resemblance to a mystery
Sometimes you'd say:
'Tell me why their clothes

Always smell of low tide?'
You began spying on us
And asking others:
'Haven't you noticed
That they're always together?
Tell me how long it's been going on?'
Soon your questions became orders
And everyone in the household
Was obliged to report
Every gesture we made
Every word we spoke.
Then came the day when you received
A visit from the pilgrims
They were like a flock
Of famished little animals
To whom you distributed crumbs
In exchange for their tattling
That day cost you dearly
And afterwards you were heard to say
That England could no longer afford
To welcome so many strangers to her shores
For fear that misery might be contagious.
In no time at all, you began looking for me:
'Where is she? Find her!
I know they're together
We must separate them
Lock him in the cellar
And as for her, burn her
No not yet
Let her live with her punishment
Let her be stigmatized
And disfigured
No wait—she is a Plantagenet

I don't want them to touch her face
I'll show clemency
We shall ask Richard
To cut off her hands.'
Then when you saw me
And judged
That I had not suffered enough
That dream you nurtured
Of having never given birth
To this girl who was taking your place
Yes that dream became reality:
'From now on Anne will be silent—
Anne will no longer be Anne.'

DUCHESS OF YORK [*fragile*] You are recreating the universe!
Why all of a sudden
Slander the purity of my kin?
We barely know you by sight.

ANNE DEXTER Because your purity is soon to die
Drowned in a cask
This house is no more than a funnel
Where everything mingles and flows
Into the rotten mouth of death
As slowly as Edward
Who's been dying since his birth
And George
Who must ask himself each morning
By what mean stroke of fate
He goes on living.
But instead of jumping for joy
He remains silent
He remains silent—not because you are there
No he is not your prisoner
No not because you appear

And force him to remain silent;
No—he stopped talking
The day you ordered me to be silent.
And to explain his silence
You lie to one and all
Sometimes claiming he is mute
Other times saying he speaks—to you
To you alone when you wish
When in fact never once
Has a single sound come out of his mouth
Since that day when you said:
'From now on Anne will be silent.'
You wanted to prevent your children from living
But look how in doing so
It is they who prevent you from dying.

DUCHESS OF YORK You prevent nothing whatsoever
Since you cannot prevent the world.
My children do not constitute the axis
Nor the rotations of the world
I am speaking of The World
Whose sole reality
Me, Cecily of England
Is soon to disappear.
Very soon, nothing of all you can see
Nothing will have any reason to exist
I shall have finally acceded
To the constitution of the universe.

ANNE DEXTER But who will mourn
A derelict in this court?
Edward and George long dead and buried?
The sisters of Warwick?
Queen Elizabeth
Deploring the loss of her orphans?

Or perhaps the Queen of Anjou
Who will die laughing?
See how your hundred years
Will quickly fall into oblivion
For lack of giving birth
To a sister for your sons
A daughter who might have been able
To mourn her mother.

DUCHESS OF YORK Not if every tear in her body
Is shed for George.

ANNE DEXTER Had you managed to transform everything
Even my heart
Into a clot of silence and oblivion
I would nevertheless continue
To ask you who is Anne.

DUCHESS OF YORK Anne …? Anne Scroop?
Anne Smith? Anne Clifford?
Anne Francoeur? Anne Maxwell?
Anne who? Our counties are full of Annes.
It's a tradition in our families
To give this Christian name
To children who will never be.
I was obliged to register your absence
And the day I learned
That you would not be born
I advised my relatives
That you would be called Anne.
How else could we possibly make sense
Of all the nothingness you constitute?

ANNE DEXTER Who is Anne?

DUCHESS OF YORK A daughter I desired
And Lord knows how I called her!
My little heart became immense

When I invoked her
But it was in vain
I went so far as to threaten her
To conjure her birth
I promised her everything she could desire
Provided that she arrive inside me
To no avail
She was not inside me
In the great beyond perhaps?
No—she was nowhere
And it would suffice
That nowhere become somewhere
To ensure that she would not be there.
Go—go—go ask them!
The Woodvilles will tell you
And the peasants in the fields
I'll grant you one hour
To speak with them
We'll say that your voice
Suddenly came back
Long enough for you
To ascertain once and for all
That Anne is nothing.
When the others tell you
Time and time again
Without a single contradiction
Perhaps you'll finally
Recognize the implacable force
Of a reality which tolerates a name
But not the woman who bears it.
Accept that she is to language
What zero is to numbers.
ANNE DEXTER Who is Anne?

DUCHESS OF YORK You ask the question
  And I repeat the answer:
  Anne is nothing.
  As sure as you exist
  As sure as you stand before my eyes
  She is nothing.
  Nothing. *Rien.*
ANNE DEXTER Who is Anne?
DUCHESS OF YORK Misery! And more misery!
  Seven times be damned!
  Who! Always who!
  Sower of who!
  What do you wish to hear?
  That George is pure love?
  No—he is nothing but silence
  Lovely stranger
  Here in the heart of London
  The desire to see you banished
  Is at the heart of my being.
ANNE DEXTER But at this very moment
  To whom are you speaking?
DUCHESS OF YORK To myself, lovely stranger, I'm saying everything
  Aloud to myself so that you can understand me.
ANNE DEXTER What would you have said to your mother
  Had she taken you for a stranger?
DUCHESS OF YORK Malice and jealousy burn in your heart
  Because you are unhappy
  You wish that I were too.
ANNE DEXTER You, living proof of your mother
  What would you have said?
  She had several children
  And counted herself amongst them.
  And when you had your own children

At first you loved them—
I still have memories
Of the woman who was my mother
She was beautiful
Mother in recognition of her children
Mother in her acts
In the tears of her early widowhood
Then intrepid dark lady on horseback
Who slashed in two the ponds
The forests and the lakes
Then attentive to the child
Who was to become king
Already dictating his government
Day in and day out
The affairs of the state
The commerce and deliveries
Never once neglecting her other children
Of which I was one, I, Anne
The child she never forgot
In the midst of endless political turmoil
The child she caressed
And taught to eat and drink
To stand up straight and courteous
To curtsey one knee to the ground
And show consideration for her brothers.

DUCHESS OF YORK This woman deserves our compassion.
A pity she abandoned you
A pity you are forced to err
Like the Spaniards.
As for me, I am dead tired
Of listening to you
And I shall attend to finding you
A more secluded place

Once peace and quiet
finally descend upon this household.
ANNE DEXTER You dare speak to me of peace
Midst this reign of confusion?

[QUEEN ELIZABETH *enters*]

QUEEN ELIZABETH Have they found my children, noble Duchess?
ANNE DEXTER Have they found her children?
Look who suddenly appears
Dishevelled but dignified
And who proclaims aloud
That she is looking for her children.
Are such things possible!
[*to* QUEEN ELIZABETH] Beware of your caresses
Beware of what you give them Elizabeth
Your children are your flesh and blood
But you mustn't love them
For giving them tender love
Will incite them to love each other
And should they manage to do so
They will find themselves like me
Condemned to silence
Their heads full of words
And hear them though they might
Over and over deep inside themselves
And hear them though you might
Over and over deep inside yourself
Those words will never
find their echo in this world
Because of a punishment
You will want to inflict upon them.
QUEEN ELIZABETH Is she insulting me?
DUCHESS OF YORK She didn't say a thing.

QUEEN ELIZABETH Have they found my children?

DUCHESS OF YORK Your children have left
  For distant lands.

QUEEN ELIZABETH Where are they?

DUCHESS OF YORK On their way to Asia.

QUEEN ELIZABETH Asia?

DUCHESS OF YORK Yes Asia
  The Asia of our dreams.

QUEEN ELIZABETH Venerable Duchess
  Each passing minute
  Threatens to carry away my king
  And plunge me into
  Irreparable desolation
  And you are telling me about your dreams?
  Where are my children?

ANNE DEXTER She is looking for them—she insists!
  She cannot imagine happiness
  Without her children.
  But, my poor Elizabeth
  How long will your love last?
  Your instinct has you looking for your children
  The way your hounds will search for bones
  Yet search as you may today
  Will you still search for them tomorrow?

QUEEN ELIZABETH See how everything drives me mad!
  Anne Dexter is standing here before me
  And I swear that I can hear her speak.

DUCHESS OF YORK Fiction Your Majesty—she is mute.

QUEEN ELIZABETH Albeit
  Order her to be silent.

[ISABEL WARWICK *comes forward*]

ISABEL WARWICK What have you done with the king, Majesty?

QUEEN ELIZABETH I made him my husband.

ISABEL WARWICK He is dying in the castle
  And you're going down to the cellars?

QUEEN ELIZABETH It is not good politics
  To leave my children in the cellars—
  The dankness of the stones
  Could damage their lungs.

ISABEL WARWICK Their lungs?

QUEEN ELIZABETH Yes their lungs—hearth of the breath of life
  And unable to flee this day
  I want to flee this place.

ISABEL WARWICK Come now, Majesty do stay.

QUEEN ELIZABETH You stay. I'm going downstairs.

ISABEL WARWICK But your health—
  Remember that the dankness …

QUEEN ELIZABETH Pardon me?

ISABEL WARWICK Remember that the dankness of the stones …

QUEEN ELIZABETH Are you the Queen of England?
  Are you the Queen of England?

ISABEL WARWICK No Majesty.

QUEEN ELIZABETH Then stay here.

  [*She exits*]

DUCHESS OF YORK [*still speaking to* ANNE DEXTER, *but changing
  her tone of voice*] We shall see each other again I hope
  'Tis a pity that you are mute
  We could have conversed you and I
  I'll wait for you here
  At four o'clock
  It is Elevation Day in this hall
  The queens have instated the custom
  To escape the monotony of their lives
  They gather here on Thursdays

To elevate themselves face to face on their little benches
They exchange compliments and observe each other
Wearing all their finery
Butterfly wings
Swan beaks
Peacock feathers
And rich and precious metals.
Your praise would be most welcome.
Who knows? Perhaps you will speak to us
Certain talents appear late
Yes you will speak
If I permit it.

[*She goes to leave.* ISABEL WARWICK *stops her*]

THE CHARIOT

ISABEL WARWICK For years now
   From this hall down to the cellars
   I travel back and forth
   Up and down night and day
   Indefatigable
   In my efforts to ensure my reign
   Only to learn today
   From the mouth of the mute woman
   That the animal I have watched grazing
   Could have spoken to me
   And what's more you love him.
   You love his stature
   And the height of his forehead
   The forehead of a warrior—and his chin
   The chin of the Plantagenets!
   Yes you love him
   But not so much as I
   Who can no longer bear
   To see him spend his days
   Facing the grey stones
   Facing the crevices, the hollow dreams
   The stony depths
   There smouldered a seething rage
   Longing to erupt
   Inside a dank cell
   As tiny as
   The furnace is enormous
   And you left him there
   His whole life long
   Repeating to one and all
   That he would gladly speak

If you so wished
One or the other of you what does it matter
'He can speak if I so desire!'
Morning noon and night
Lord he was talkative!
Oh no one expressed himself
As clearly as he
When happy he roared
Unhappy he yelped
And having spent an hour
Listening to my confessions
The future King of England
Would wallow in his fill of hay
I might as well have gone to the stables
To chat with our horses.
His reign promised
To be exalting for you
Who would have ruled over our island
Ordering the king
First to speak
Then to remain silent!
You laughed poor Duchess
You dreamed a great deal
And I was a silly goose
Who knew next to nothing
Your son can use his voice
To fabricate words!
He is not so different in nature from you
And I am nothing
Nothing but a two-legged spouse
Made for running up and down stairs
Up and down down and up without cease
Weakened in the name of power

While unbeknownst to me
He speaks to you as a human being!
And Anne Dexter! She speaks too!
Where is her voice let me hear it again!
What is it like? Is it shrill?
Forty pence I wager that her voice is hoarse!
What do they say to each other?
What does the man say to her
What does the animal hide from me?
Instead of having hands
Could she possibly have a heart?
The heart of a human being?
Good Lord all I need now
Is to discover her image
In the mirror of calm waters
When I contemplate myself!
Listen and show some respect!
I am talking to you Duchess
I am the most powerful
I too can speak listen to me
Queen to be and for years to come
Queen the wife of George
Queen at the centre my subjects gathered round.
To better manage imports and commerce
The ships on the Thames all mine
The animals the produce mine
The shearing mine the increase
The acceleration of merchandise
The acquisition of metals
The perfection of England
Quickly before day's end
So that tomorrow I may take over Scotland
That my continent may vibrate

And your reputations go up in flames
For I intend to use your ashes
They will be useful for God knows what
As everything will have a use
And dead you'll undoubtedly be more useful
Than living as you are now
Dazed and dumbfounded
While I speak at last.
I wish to say here in London
That I have come
From the House of Warwick
With my two hands
Unencumbered by rings or baggage
With nothing but
My own two hands ...

[QUEEN ELIZABETH *enters*]

QUEEN ELIZABETH ... And with your sister
    Isabel Warwick
    Your misbegotten sister
    Come to flatter Richard
    With one hand versed in sweetness
    And the other set to slay the innocents.
    Ah ... Ah ... what a sight!
    You see me so distraught
    I must strive to understand
    How what we are experiencing
    Is not a dream.
    I was groping in the dark
    Having lost my torch
    When suddenly
    On the surface of a cask ...
    [*abruptly*] Anne Warwick!

VOICE OF ANNE WARWICK Majesty?

QUEEN ELIZABETH Have you seen to the rebate on the deliveries?

VOICE OF ANNE WARWICK I'm on my way Majesty.

QUEEN ELIZABETH I asked you to see to it an hour ago!

VOICE OF ANNE WARWICK Yes Majesty.

QUEEN ELIZABETH Anne Warwick
　　How fares the king?

VOICE OF ANNE WARWICK He fares little
　　Though he is talking

QUEEN ELIZABETH What is he saying?

VOICE OF ANNE WARWICK He is dictating his will.

QUEEN ELIZABETH Again?

VOICE OF ANNE WARWICK It seems that he forgot someone.

QUEEN ELIZABETH Who might that be?

VOICE OF ANNE WARWICK Someone who has rights to the inheritance.

QUEEN ELIZABETH Who?

VOICE OF ANNE WARWICK A certain Jane Shore
　　Who it is said …

QUEEN ELIZABETH [*beside herself*] Jane Shore!

VOICE OF ANNE WARWICK A most esteemed lady
　　Like blue skies in London
　　She knows the kings well
　　And the paupers have faith in her
　　The beauty of her features
　　Leads them to believe that she is queen
　　At the head of an empire
　　Where hearts are her subjects
　　Her smile is worth
　　A kingdom so they say …

QUEEN ELIZABETH Jane Shore mistress to the kings
　　Born simple-minded as sure as I am queen
　　But on a bright and sunny day
　　Wife without scruples of a goldsmith

Who waits for her all evening long
And cajoles her when she returns
And deposits on their bed
Which she has royally betrayed
The entire inheritance of the Woodvilles
And that of the Plantagenets
Venerable Duchess
Yes poor Duchess
Your belongings and mine
Are down there on Welford Street
In the oil-stained hands
Of Jane Shore's husband
While I run to Edward's bedside
To bathe his feverish brow
And brighten his days
And conjure for him
Cheerful images of the afterlife
Till I no longer know what to invent
And lose sight of my children
Till I forget that they were even born.

[*Pause*]

I came upstairs for something ... ah!
Death has descended upon us
Richard has killed George
I saw his heart torn out
And I saw his two black eyes
The horror is such
That Edward would seem in fine health
And Margaret's hideous countenance
Would find itself dethroned.
ISABEL WARWICK George is alive Majesty.
QUEEN ELIZABETH No Isabel Warwick

Go downstairs and see for yourself
George has been assassinated.

ISABEL WARWICK [*radiant*] Ha! That will teach me a lesson
It scarcely took an hour
Till by word of mouth
My strategy travelled round the castle!
And I had simply come looking for a glove!

QUEEN ELIZABETH But didn't you go downstairs to look?

ISABEL WARWICK Yes Majesty
At least I went as far as his door
And I closed it tight
For fear that someone might come
And notice he was still alive.

QUEEN ELIZABETH For naught since he was dead
And how great your pain will be
When you see that …

ISABEL WARWICK It will never be sharper
Than an hour ago!
Speaking of that glove …

QUEEN ELIZABETH [*shaking her*] Come to your senses and don't leave
me here alone
Have pity on me! I feel so isolated from everyone.

ISABEL WARWICK And who is to blame?
Isolation is something one wishes upon oneself.

QUEEN ELIZABETH What did I wish upon myself?
Edward's death perhaps?

ISABEL WARWICK He is not dead yet
Nor are your children.
What has become of hope?
Instead of flaunting my sorrows
I allowed myself to act and look
George will finally get to reign.

QUEEN ELIZABETH Quite a reign believe me!

I saw him in the cask.

ISABEL WARWICK Ha! At the bottom? Or on the surface?

QUEEN ELIZABETH Two huge black eyes …

ISABEL WARWICK Yes—'his blood, his eyes'
    You are repeating my very words!

QUEEN ELIZABETH Go downstairs Isabel Warwick
    I order you to do so.

ISABEL WARWICK You …

QUEEN ELIZABETH Are you the Queen of England?

ISABEL WARWICK Not yet Majesty.

QUEEN ELIZABETH Then obey me.

[ISABEL WARWICK *exits in the direction of the cellars.* QUEEN
MARGARET *enters with the children and collapses onto her baggage*]

QUEEN ELIZABETH But those are my children!
    Ah I have found you o my angels!
    How cold your hands are!
    And your foreheads!
    Have you noticed the tinyness of their nails?
    I love you
    God willing may my life
    Magically reverse its course
    And take me back forever
    To the happiness of childhood.
    I love you, I love you.
    Come here, that I might save you!

[*The bells strike three*]

Three o'clock already?
Margaret, what time is it?
What? You are here in London?
And so am I—and all of us!
Elevation Day, I had forgotten!

Take them I entrust them to you
Venerable Duchess
Take them to a chamber
Behind closed doors
And see that Anne Warwick
Is never allowed to approach them.
Farewell my princes.
DUCHESS OF YORK Isn't Anne Warwick in Scotland?
QUEEN ELIZABETH No alas
I'm afraid she won't leave London so readily.
DUCHESS OF YORK Farewell I am taking them with me
However lowly be their shelter
Their eyes will make four stars
A sign of glory.

[*The* DUCHESS OF YORK *exits with the children in the direction of the castle*]

QUEEN MARGARET Everything has disappeared
All that remains of what the kings erected
Is the dungeon in our tower
Which appears like the mast
Of an old ship
Adrift in the middle of a circle
There is no more land
No more water no more horizon
Asia, that I longed to see
Too far east of the winds
Which wage their war upon us
Is evermore distant
And here I am again
Survivor of the winds
The snows the steppes.
At the outset I went by sea

It was agitated
But less tormented than I.
After an hour or two
Or perhaps a long month later
For living is arduous business
I disembarked at the foot of enormous cliffs
The cliffs of Russia.
I suddenly believed these children
Were going to stop living
So I did a turnabout
To protect them from the gales
Then, back to the wind
I began to retreat, hastily
Heading towards the Orient.
But on that fateful day
There were countless whirlwinds
Which spun me about in semi-circles.
I saw Turks and Cypriots
African slaves
Each tribe showed me the way to China
But all was lies
Because, sure that Asia
Was looming up behind me
It was towards London—I realize now
That I was retreating
London London
Why so much hesitation
When comes the time to dream of leaving?
'Tis the very globe
Which disappears within us
So totally that
Disparate
Non-English

In discord but nevertheless
That I may recognize you
Unequal you
You recognize me
If possible
If you can, could
Possible that
My obscure dignity
I, by compassion
Re-establish.

ANNE WARWICK *enters, breathless*

ANNE WARWICK Through what door does Richard usually enter?
QUEEN ELIZABETH This one.
   Why do you ask?
ANNE WARWICK Is there any means of
   Digging a hole
   And crawling into the cellars?
QUEEN ELIZABETH Such means are hardly noble.
ANNE WARWICK Ah perhaps.
QUEEN ELIZABETH You must be dreaming
   That Richard is crawling at your feet.
ANNE WARWICK Yes perhaps.
QUEEN ELIZABETH 'Ah perhaps. Yes perhaps.'
   Perhaps you've given yourself away?

   [*Death knell*]

ANNE WARWICK Listen Majesty
   The bells of the Abbey are tolling.
QUEEN ELIZABETH Edward, my God …
QUEEN MARGARET Edward!
QUEEN ELIZABETH [*tearing out her hair*] No more ornaments!
   May a stark desert crown my head!
ANNE WARWICK Madam Woodville, was it your children
   I saw in the arms of the Duchess?
QUEEN ELIZABETH Yes perhaps.
ANNE WARWICK Why did you give them to her?
QUEEN ELIZABETH To protect them from your ambition
   Anne Warwick
   Misbegotten—hydrocephalic urchin.
ANNE WARWICK It seems to me that you had

A husband who became king
And two children by this king
If your happiness was incomplete
You alone must have withheld
Whatever was missing.

QUEEN ELIZABETH Enough of your sarcasm
I would never tolerate it
Even if life had granted me
A certain happiness in reigning
But I paid for having
What deprived me of my contented lot
And I am still paying
By enduring the fear of losing all.
Aren't you afraid Anne Warwick
That your superiority
Will finally make you dizzy?
I hope at least
That you know yourself well.

ANNE WARWICK My sister of Warwick would tell you
That at my age—twelve—

QUEEN ELIZABETH You lie to us about your age.

ANNE WARWICK ... At my age—twelve—
Knowledge vacillates
Between the known and the unknown.

QUEEN ELIZABETH Aaaaah! Enough be silent—
Your sister! Your sister!
Look at your sister
Who believed she had risen above us.
Why don't you go
Console her in her sorrows?

ANNE WARWICK Worse sorrows are yet to come.

QUEEN ELIZABETH Name them.

ANNE WARWICK I cannot name them all.

QUEEN ELIZABETH Name the ones you know.

ANNE WARWICK Richard.

QUEEN ELIZABETH Richard!

ANNE WARWICK He asked me ...

QUEEN ELIZABETH Asked you what?

ANNE WARWICK To bring him your children
    So that he could kill them—
    And I did it.

QUEEN ELIZABETH Oh no! You are lying
    Anne Warwick, no! no!
    How can I believe you?
    You couldn't possibly have torn my children
    Out of the arms of the Duchess.

ANNE WARWICK She entrusted them to me Majesty—
    She is so confused!

QUEEN ELIZABETH You are lying you are delirious.

ANNE WARWICK My sister couldn't believe
    That George had died assassinated.
    Now you must look upon your children
    As if they were only legends
    It is our life or theirs.

QUEEN ELIZABETH [*voraciously*] Theirs! Theirs at all costs!
    Here, take all I have
    Everything you want
    Edward's bed, my ornaments
    My stags and my hounds
    Daring, alert, priceless
    Those airy mastiffs
    They watch us
    With eyes so voluptuous
    You think you see
    A dream unfolding
    They leap between the forests

And dash through the mist
They are more splendid
Than all the stars in Ireland
Upstairs in my coffers I have
Pearls from the deep sea
Some fallen from the moon
They can influence our tears
I give them all to you
Take them Anne Warwick
I possess treasures
Unknown to all the tribes on earth
I have birds for you
The likes of which you've never seen
In my ponds I breed fish
Their fins are golden filaments
I have stones Anne Warwick
Pure stones known only unto me
You need only consult them
To predict the plagues
The fires and all manner of disaster
And destruction
My talismans I give them all to you
More than you dared covet in your dreams
Secrets you cannot
Reveal even to yourself
All that is mine I give to you
Tools of bronze
Powders to concoct colours
Instruments which teach us
To fathom the bed of the Thames
Truths to which I alone am privy
Truths which can humiliate our enemies
I am prepared to display it all

Everything, before your eyes
But give me back my children.

ANNE WARWICK All that you were
And all that you had belongs to me
Except two children
A fiction born some hours ago
In the tumultuous belly
Of your imagination.

QUEEN ELIZABETH You have to get them back from Richard.

ANNE WARWICK Listen ... your enemy
The wind is calling you Majesty.

QUEEN ELIZABETH Edward ...
Run and tell Richard ...
No wait ...
They are on their way to Asia
You couldn't have ...
You had no right ...
Anne Warwick, what right did you have?
You must resuscitate them!

[ISABEL WARWICK *enters, overwhelmed with grief*]

ISABEL WARWICK [*to* ANNE WARWICK] Go—you can tell Richard
They have already killed George.

[*She collapses*]

THE DEATH OF THE DUCHESS

Four o'clock

QUEEN MARGARET Already?
  What you just found out?
  Why did no one ask me?
  For twenty-four hours
  No, for the last two days
  Two days?—two weeks
  Two months two years two centuries
  I've seen him lying dead in that cask
  This is ancient history
  A story I had already ceased
  To enjoy
  I was much too impatient
  To see how long
  His brother Edward would survive him.
  Edward our sovereign
  Our lord and our everything
  Our King Edward has finally died!
  Oh such a long death!
  I had time to travel to Russia
  And time to return to London
  While he gasped his final breath!
  Stand up poor Elizabeth
  Stand up Isabel Warwick
  The death knell is no longer tolling
  Listen—listen
  The carillon in the belltower is striking
  Four o'clock
  Let us delay our sorrows
  It is the hour of the Elevation

Which I proclaim to be open
On this Thursday January twentieth
In the year one thousand four hundred eighty-three.
Let us rise.

[*She climbs the stairs*]

There is no carillon so pure
As the sound of our pearls
Your gown Elizabeth
Becomes your power
Oh so much gold Isabel
All draped in fire!
As for your skin
The scent of Thursday
Makes me faint with intoxication.

[*The* DUCHESS OF YORK *enters with the children in her arms*]

DUCHESS OF YORK Here comes the night—
The evil of daytime
Will be transformed into good.
I shall reappear in you
My supreme little children
For I am a harp
And you are its strings.

[*She notices* ANNE WARWICK]

Anne Warwick, my pure beauty
Are you really here in London?
Look see who I am
See our birthright
Who we are.
ANNE WARWICK I am the wife of King Richard III
Her Majesty Queen Anne of England.

Madam Woodville
Have you seen to the rebate on the deliveries?
DUCHESS OF YORK Yes God save the Queen
 And me Cecily of London
 Anne, before I die
 By your will may the impossible come true.
ANNE WARWICK The impossible so soon?
DUCHESS OF YORK Lend me your crown.
ANNE WARWICK It belongs to me.
DUCHESS OF YORK Lend it to me.
ANNE WARWICK I have accomplished many exploits
 In order to feel its weight.
DUCHESS OF YORK I would like to wear it for ten seconds.
ANNE WARWICK Ten seconds is very little.
DUCHESS OF YORK I gave the world to Richard
 And I am leaving life
 I beg of you
 Imagine the pain of having lived a hundred years
 Imagine that having arrived this far you will say
 'My life, already unfolded?'
 Ten seconds is very little
 But a century is nothing
 I would like to have the illusion
 In honour of my departure
 Of having been, of being
 I Cecily, queen of this empire.
ANNE WARWICK Is reigning for so little time worth the trouble?
DUCHESS OF YORK Anne.

 [*Pause*]

 I beg of you.
 Look, I am lowering myself
 Must I really

Bend both my old knees to the ground?
ANNE WARWICK All for a lie?
DUCHESS OF YORK Our life on this earth is a lie—
Shreds that we are.

[*She tries to kneel but falls.* ANNE WARWICK *hesitates, then consents to lend her the crown in exchange for the children. A long silence. The* DUCHESS OF YORK *places the crown on her head and reigns for ten seconds, her eyes closed. Then she puts the crown back on* ANNE WARWICK'*s head*]

DUCHESS OF YORK [*dying*] Thank you.
ANNE WARWICK If you wish
I can loan it to you
A few moments more.
DUCHESS OF YORK That would be too long
I reigned ten seconds
And I saw what I wanted to see
I elevated myself
Above the pitiful fate of the world
And I had the fleeting impression
That I could correct it
I towered so high I found
My century minute
And could speak to it for what it's worth
And for what its children will be worth
My destiny allowed me
To reign before dying
So that I might see with these eyes
Almost a hundred years old
That there is nothing behind us
And that everything lies ahead
My life is ending and the New World begins
The universe was imprisoned in my breath

Now I exhale at last
And I release it all
The hounds, the stags
The birds and the does
The moon oh the marvel
The glow!

NORMAND CHAURETTE was born in Montreal in 1954. Plays published by Leméac Éditeur include: *Rêve d'une nuit d'hôpital* (1980); *Provincetown Playhouse, juillet 1919, j'avais 19 ans* (1981), translated by William Boulet for the anthology *Quebec Voices* (Coach House Press, 1986); *Fêtes d'automne* (1986); *La Société de Métis* (1983); *Fragments d'une lettre d'adieu lus par des géologues* (1986), nominated for the 1987 Governor General's Award and the Prix de l'Association québécoise des critiques de théâtre for the Best Play Produced in 1988, and translated by Linda Gaboriau as *Fragments of a Farewell Letter Read by Geologists* (1989); *Les Reines* (1991). He has also published a novel, *Scènes d'enfants*, which was nominated for the 1989 Governor General's Award. His plays have been showcased or produced in Montreal, Toronto, Winnipeg, Banff, New York, Paris, Brussels, and Florence, as well as in Zaire and the Congo. His most recent plays have been translated into English and Italian.

LINDA GABORIAU was born in Boston and moved to Montreal in 1963 where she completed B.A. and M.A. degrees in French Language and Literature at McGill University. She has been active in Canadian and Quebec theatre for twenty years as a critic, journalist, broadcaster and consultant. Her translations of more than thirty plays include the works of some of Quebec's most prominent playwrights. Her translation of Michel Marc Bouchard's *Les Feluettes*, published as *Lilies* by Coach House Press, was nominated for the 1991 Governor General's Award for literary translation, and won both the 1990-1991 Dora Mavor Moore Award for Outstanding New Play and a 1992 Chalmers Award for an outstanding Canadian play.